JUL 31 2013

A Green Kid's Guide to
Gardening!

A Green Kid's Guide to
Garden Pest Removal

by Richard Lay
illustrated by Laura Zarrin

magic
Wagon

Published by Magic Wagon, a division of the ABDO Publishing Group, PO Box 398166, Minneapolis, Minnesota, 55439. Copyright © 2013 by Abdo Consulting Group, Inc. International copyrights reserved in all countries. All rights reserved. No part of this book may be reproduced in any form without written permission from the publisher.

Looking Glass Library™ is a trademark and logo of Magic Wagon.

Printed in the United States of America, North Mankato, MN.
102012
012013
 This book contains at least 10% recycled materials.

Text by Richard Lay
Illustrations by Laura Zarrin
Edited by Stephanie Hedlund and Rochelle Baltzer
Interior layout and design by Renée LaViolette
Cover design by Renée LaViolette

Library of Congress Cataloging-in-Publication Data
Lay, Richard.
  A green kid's guide to garden pest removal / by Richard Lay ; illustrated by Laura Zarrin.
     p. cm. -- (A green kid's guide to gardening!)
  Includes index.
  ISBN 978-1-61641-944-8
  1. Garden pests--Control--Juvenile literature. I. Zarrinnaal, Laura Nienhaus. II. Title. III. Series: Lay, Richard. Green kid's guide to gardening!
  SB603.5.L39 2013
  635.9'2--dc23
                          2012023790

Table of Contents

Say No to Poison!

A gardener is a person who grows plants. "Being green" means learning how to live on Earth without hurting it. Green gardeners grow plants and protect Earth at the same time.

All gardens are like a finger with a splinter. They have things that do not belong there. They have bugs. Some gardeners use poisons called pesticides to get rid of bugs. But, pesticides kill all bugs.

Green gardeners say no to pesticides that kill all bugs. They know that some bugs are good. A green gardener works to keep good bugs. He or she only gets rid of bad bugs.

Good Bugs, Bad Bugs

A garden needs bees and butterflies. These are good bugs. A fruit or vegetable plant has flowers. These flowers have seeds called pollen. Pollen is used to make fruit. But the pollen must go to another flower.

Bees and butterflies eat pollen from the flowers. Some of the pollen gets on their legs. When they fly to another flower, they drop the pollen into the flower. The flower uses the new pollen to make fruit.

Other bugs are bad. They hurt plants. Some eat leaves. Others suck the food or water from plants. If you do not use pesticides, how do you get rid of bad bugs, like squash bugs and aphids?

Use Your Hands

A green gardener finds other ways to get rid of bugs instead of using pesticides. First, they use their hands to get rid of bugs. Look under the leaves where bugs like to hide. Then, pick them off and drop them into a dish of soapy water. But, be sure to wear gloves. Insects can bite.

Green gardeners also use a water hose to remove pests. They put a nozzle on the end of a hose and spray the plants. This knocks off the bugs. It will not hurt the plants.

Bug Secrets

A green gardener learns secrets about insects. For example, insects are picky eaters. Each bug will only eat a few types of plants. If you grow different plants close together, the smells will be mixed up. This will confuse the bugs and they will not go there.

Insects are easily tricked. Every year plant your vegetables in a new place. The bugs will go back to the place you used last year. They will not find their food.

Insects give up quickly. If they cannot get to the fruit, they will move on. You can wrap cantaloupe in the legs of a woman's pantyhose. It will not stop the fruit from growing or getting air. But, it will stop beetles from getting to the fruit.

The Enemy of My Enemy

Nature has given the gardener many friends. Bugs have enemies that a green gardener wants in the garden.

Birds and bats eat bugs. All the birds in your backyard eat bugs. Bats are great bug eaters. A colony of bats will eat millions of bugs in a year. Many green gardeners build bird or bat houses near their gardens.

Frogs and toads also eat bugs. They love to hide under the leaves in your garden. They also love that your garden is a wet place. Take the time to build a frog house to welcome this critter.

Good bugs eat bad bugs. For example, ladybugs will eat aphids. Aphids hurt tomatoes and beans. You can buy ladybugs at many garden stores.

Many green gardeners put flowers in their garden to draw good bugs. Good bugs such as ladybugs, small wasps, and lacewings love wildflowers and sunflowers. They also like the flowers on marigolds and rosemary.

Ants Hate Mint!

Insects don't like certain plants. A green gardener will put plants in the garden that drive bugs away.

For example, ants hate mint. Insects also do not like onions. Onions and garlic keep away aphids and most beetles. Squash bugs will not come around radishes.

Rosemary will keep out most flies and moths. The smellier the plant, the more it drives away bad bugs.

If You Must

There are some chemicals a green gardener can use that are not pesticides. For example, mix dishwasher soap and water and spray it on plants to kill aphids.

Garlic and chili peppers kill insects. Cut up these two vegetables and mix them with water in a spray bottle. Spray this on your plants.

Finally, green gardeners can use neem oil. An adult must help to use this. Mix the oil with water and spray it on the plants. Neem oil makes the insects think they are not hungry. They will stop eating.

If you use neem oil, do not spray it in the morning or evening. Bees and butterflies eat during those times. It will also keep them from eating.

Keep the Good Ones

Green gardeners keep bad bugs out. But they also grow plants to bring in good bugs. They build houses for birds, bats, and frogs. They can also plant vegetables that bad bugs hate.

A green gardener does not use pesticides. Be a green gardener and look for bad bugs every day. If you see them, pick them off or use soap and water to get rid of them. If that does not work, try other green ways to send them away without using harmful chemicals.

Build a Frog House

You will need:
A large plastic flowerpot
Markers
Leaves or straw

Steps to making a frog house:

1. Use the markers to decorate half of the pot.
2. Go to the garden and find a shady spot.
3. Dig a hole the width of the pot when it is on its side. Dig down about 5 to 7 inches (13 to 18 cm).
4. Place the pot on its side in the hole. Make sure your decorations are on top.
5. Fill the pot halfway with dirt and leaves or straw. Make sure there is room for the frog to climb in.
6. Wait for a frog to come enjoy its new home!

Glossary

neem oil: oil from the neem tree of India. Its oil is used to remove insects from plants.

pesticide: chemicals used to kill insects.

pollen: the tiny, yellow grains of flowers.

trellis: a frame of crisscrossing bars that supports climbing plants.

Web Sites

To learn more about green gardening, visit ABDO Group online. Web sites about green gardening are featured on our Book Links page. These links are routinely monitored and updated to provide the most current information available. www.abdopublishing.com

Index